ourney.....................

MONGOLIA

Gobi Desert

Lop

CHINA

Shangtu

Peking

JAPAN

AYAS

TIBET

Hangchow

Zayton

BURMA

YUNNAN

MALAY PENINSULAR

South
China Sea

CEYLON

THE TRAVELS OF

Marco Polo

Bernard Brett

COLLINS

HANC QUAM VIDEGIS
DESCRIDSIT DELINEAVITQUE
SIVE DE BELLO DICTUS

GERRARUM ORBIS TABULAM
RICHRDUS DE HALDINGHAM
A S CIRCA MCCC

ISBN 0 00 192243 2
First published 1971
Reprinted 1973
© *Text and illustrations Bernard Brett 1971*
Printed in Great Britain by William Collins Sons & Co. Ltd, Glasgow

Introduction

This is how the world was thought to be in 1280, during Marco Polo's lifetime. The "Mappa Mundi" or map of the world, which is in Hereford Cathedral, shows very little of Asia, and is wildly inaccurate. It was not until the famous travels of Marco Polo that the maps of this area began to resemble those we know today. But a hundred years passed before map makers began to include Marco's findings.

The map attached to the end papers shows the journeys made by Marco, his father Nicolo and his uncle Maffeo. The book should be read together with the map, so that you can trace the places visited as you read. The importance of Marco Polo's travels lies in the fact that, at a time when men in Europe knew little of the remainder of the world, he made an immense journey into the unknown leaving behind him a record of the people and the strange sights he saw. He also encouraged others, including Christopher Columbus, to follow in his footsteps.

roduced by kind permission of The Dean and Chapter of Hereford Cathedral

The Story of Marco Polo

The Doge, chief magistrate of Venice

Who was Marco Polo? We know he was born in Venice in the year 1254, the son of Nicolo Polo, a merchant with trading interests in Constantinople, but we know nothing of his boyhood.

When Marco was still a child his father and Uncle Maffeo, being cut off by a Tartar war whilst trading in the Crimea, decided to journey eastwards. After travelling several thousand miles they eventually arrived at Peking, the capital of Kublai Khan, the ruler of the Tartars. The Khan treated them kindly, sending them back to Europe with a message for the Pope, requesting that the Polos should return with a hundred Christian missionaries.

Finding on his return to Venice that his wife had died, Nicolo decided to take his son, Marco, now seventeen years old, with him on his return journey to China. The Pope, Gregory X, could only let them have two preaching friars, who accompanied them as far as Armenia, but rumours of a war frightened the friars into returning. The Venetians travelled on for over three years, arriving at the Khan's court in 1275. Kublai made much of Marco who, quickly learning the language and customs of the Tartars, was sent as an administrator to many wild parts of the Khan's Empire. Marco made careful note of all the strange customs he saw.

After seventeen years spent in the service of Kublai Khan, the Polos were eager to return to Venice, but the Khan would not allow them to leave. However, it chanced at this time, that envoys from the Khan of Persia arrived at Peking, to seek the hand in marriage of the Tartar Princess Cocachin for their master.

The overland route to Persia being unsafe because of wars among the Tartars, the envoys decided to make the return journey with the Princess by sea, begging that the Polos should be allowed to go with them, "as being people well skilled in the practice of navigation".

Reluctantly the Khan agreed, and in 1292 a splendid convoy set out from the port of Zayton, with the Venetians carrying the golden tablet of Kublai for safe conduct.

After a voyage lasting two years the Polos arrived in Persia, where they learned that both Kublai Khan and the Khan of Persia had died. The new Khan of Persia, after receiving the Princess Cocachin, speeded the Venetians on their way, with a troop of horsemen for protection. They finally reached Venice in 1295, to find the city at war with Genoa.

Marco spent only a short time with his relatives, before sailing with a Venetian fleet that was defeated by the Genoese; he was captured and remained a prisoner in Genoa for three years. During his imprisonment he dictated the story of his travels to a fellow prisoner, Rusticiano of Pisa. Marco returned to Venice in 1299, but little more is known of him until his death in 1324. However, the book of his travels remains, giving us a glowing picture of the wonders of the East, although he, himself, said, "I have not written down the half of these things which I saw, for I knew I would not be believed". Polo inspired many to follow in his footsteps; for example, Christopher Columbus, when he sailed west in the *Santa Maria*, carried a well-thumbed copy of Marco's book with him.

Marco Polo telling his story

Venice

Many centuries before, barbarians from the north had invaded Italy, driving some of the people to seek refuge in a group of marshy islands in the Adriatic. Here they founded Venice, a city with canals instead of roads. At the time of Marco Polo, Venice, "Bride of the Adriatic" was at the height of her power, her warehouses filled with costly merchandise from all over the known world. The silks, spices and jade from the Near and Far East were passed from one country to another, often taking years on the way. Thus, until the Polos went on their great journeys, the merchants who carried them the last few hundred miles knew nothing of the lands from which they originally came.

When Nicolo and Maffeo Polo returned to Venice, after an absence of fifteen years, they found Marco eager to accompany them on their return journey to China.

The Voyage to Acre

Crossbowman and seaman of the period

In 1271 a Venetian galley slowly glided over the lagoon to the open sea; sails were hoisted, and so began one of the most important adventures in history. After a stay of only two years, the Polo brothers were once again returning to China; this time they had with them the seventeen-year-old Marco.

Their galley was long and narrow, built both for speed and fighting. Banked on either side with long oars, it had a tall mast and lateen-rigged sail; two great side oars were used to steer the ship. They sailed in convoy, Venetian fashion, carrying crossbowmen and archers as a defence against the fierce pirates who prowled the Mediterranean. Crews were hired for the shipping season, March 1st to November 30th, freemen over the age of eighteen who had sworn an oath of allegiance to Venice.

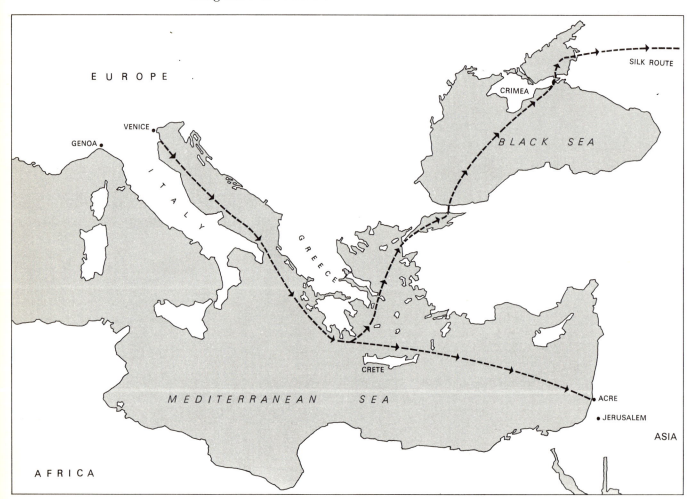

The location of Venice established it as a great trading centre between east and west. Eastern countries sent goods by caravan to Constantinople or Acre and then by ship up the Adriatic to Venice. Venice was also the meeting point of the European trade routes; merchandise from France, Germany, the Baltic, and the Low Countries poured into the city to be shipped across the sea to the eastern ports

Sailing into Acre

The food on the voyage was simple: salt meat, cheese, onions, garlic and vinegar, the passengers supplying their own water, wine, cooking utensils and firewood. Venetian Law forbade the frying of fish in order to prevent fire at sea.

Steering by the newly invented magnetic "nedylle" and the stars, they nosed their way through the Adriatic, on past Corfu to Acre. They were at sea for forty days; endless days of seasickness, heat, bad food, sour wine and cramped living quarters!

At Acre the travellers met a priest called Theobald, who was later to become Pope Gregory X. He found them two Dominican friars, who were willing to make the journey to China, a far cry from the hundred requested by Kublai Khan.

Armed with a letter to the Khan from the new Pope, they set out on the long overland journey across Asia.

The Fountain of Oil

Marco and his companions, travelling sometimes on foot, sometimes on horseback or by camel, slowly made their way eastward. As they passed through Armenia into Persia, they saw and heard of many wonders. Marco made careful note of everything he encountered.

He tells of natural baths of warm water, and he seemed fascinated by a fountain of oil which gushed from the ground, day and night without ceasing. He described it as ". . . a fountain of oil which discharges so great a quantity as to furnish loading for many camels. The purpose of it is not for food, but as an unguent for cutaneous distempers in men and cattle . . . and it is also good for burning". This place is now known as the Baku oilfields in southern Russia, and provides millions of gallons of oil every year.

Marco learned of many local legends. One of these referred to Noah's Ark, which he was assured could be seen on top of a high mountain called Mount Ararat, near the Turkish town of Erzurum. Left behind by the flood, it rested there still amidst the eternal snows of the summit.

People of the Middle East

Turkish merchant

Throughout his travels Marco took a lively interest in the manners and customs of all the people he met; their crafts, trades and general way of life.

The people of Lesser Armenia he describes as Christians, but not very good Christians, for they are not "as the Romans are". They were once brave soldiers, but now "they are without any good qualities, but are the best sort of drinkers".

In Anatolia, "the Turcomans, who reverence Mahomet and follow his law, are a rude people, and dull of intellect. They live amongst the mountains and in places difficult of access, where their object is to find good pasture for their cattle".

Georgia produces people who are, "well made, bold sailors and expert archers". Women of Tunocain, according to Marco, "were the most beautiful in the world".

Persian soldier

Woman of Kerman, weaving

13

Baghdad

Marco described Baghdad, the city of the Caliphs as, ". . . the noblest and most extensive city to be found in this part of the world". At this time it was famous for its ". . . silks wrought with gold, and also damasks, as well as of velvets ornamented with the figures of birds and beasts".

　　Here he heard the story of the capture of Baghdad by Haluga, Khan of the Levant. Haluga discovered that the Caliph had amassed great treasure, but spent no money on soldiers to defend it. The Khan's army, consisting of a hundred thousand horsemen, besides foot soldiers, overran the city. To teach the Caliph a lesson, Haluga locked him in a tower and told him to eat his gold if he could; Marco concludes, "there in the midst of his wealth, he soon finished a miserable existence"

Animals Encountered

Marco tells of many animals and birds, unknown in Europe at that time. Here are some of them, together with his descriptions:

The Zebu, a breed of cattle still common today
"Among the cattle also there are some of an uncommon kind, particularly a species of large white oxen, with short, smooth coats, horns short, thick and obtuse, and having between the shoulders a gibbous rising or bump, about the height of two palms."

Large Sheep
". . . sheep that are equal to the ass in size, with long thick tails, weighing thirty pounds and upward, which are fat and excellent to eat."

Moufflon

"*In this plain [Kashmir] there are wild animals in great numbers, particularly sheep of a large size, having horns, three, four and even six palms in length. Of these the shepherds form ladles and vessels for holding their victuals.*"

Yaks

"*. . . many wild cattle that, in point of size, may be compared to elephants. Their colour is a mixture of white and black, and they are very beautiful to the sight. The hair on every part of their bodies lies down smooth, excepting upon the shoulder, where it stands up to the height of about three palms. Their hair or wool is white and more soft and delicate than silk.*"

Attack by Caruanas

At Kerman the road branched. The northern route to the East lay
through Afghanistan and across the fearsome Gobi Desert. Marco's
father decided on the southern route, which would take them to
Hormuz, a port on the Persian Gulf, and then by sea round India.

For safety they joined a large group of travellers journeying together
in a caravan (as it is called) which was also travelling south. The road
to Hormuz passed through wild and mountainous country, haunted

by a fierce bandit tribe called the Caruanas. Marco had heard that
these robbers practised magic and sorcery, being able to create swirling
dust fogs, from which they could pounce upon unsuspecting travellers.

The bandits finally did attack; taken completely by surprise, the
caravan scattered in all directions. The Venetians and most of their
party escaped to the nearby castle of Konsalmi, but the other members
of the caravan were either murdered or sold into slavery.

A ship of Hormuz

Hormuz

The port of Hormuz was reached without further incident. The Polos found it crowded with sailors and merchants from every part of Asia, wrangling over the price of spices, pearls, elephant tusks, silks and other merchandise.

Riverside Huts

In summer the intense heat drove the inhabitants to the banks of a nearby river, where they lived in huts built over the water: Marco writes, "here they reside during the period in which there blows every day, from about the hour of nine until noon, a land-wind (Simoon) so intensely hot as to impede respiration; and to occasion death by suffocating the person exposed to it. As soon as the approach of this wind is perceived by the inhabitants, they immerge themselves to the chin in water and continue in that situation until it ceases to blow".

As proof of this, Marco claims to have been in Hormuz when an enemy army from Kerman, consisting of sixteen hundred horsemen and five thousand foot soldiers, were caught in this fearful wind. Suffocated to a man, their bodies became so brittle that they crumbled to dust when the people of Hormuz tried to bury them.

But Nicolo was bitterly disappointed with the ships he saw, which Marco describes as, ". . . of the worst kind, and dangerous for navigation". They were made of a wood so hard and brittle, that it was impossible to drive in nails without cracking it like earthenware. The planks had to be bored and fastened together with wooden pins, and then bound with rope made from the husks of coconuts. "They were also small, having only one mast, and no iron anchors, were often driven ashore in bad weather and lost."

Marco's father decided it would be safer to return to Kerman and take the overland route to China.

Deserts

Three days' march from Kerman saw the Venetians at the edge of a great salt desert, one of the many deserts they were to cross before they reached Peking. Marco says of this particular one, "during the first three days but little water is to be met with, and that little is impregnated with salt, green as grass, and so nauseous that none can use it as drink". A later explorer talks of ". . . crossing a river of liquid salt, so deep as to take my horse up to the knees; the surface of the plain for several hundred yards on each side was entirely hid by a thick encrustation of white salt, resembling a fall of frozen snow, that crackled under the horses' hooves".

After this, they crossed further terrible deserts, until they came to the Gobi, the last and most terrible of all, guarding the way to Peking.

Here they remained for a week to rest and prepare themselves for the crossing. Marco found that to cross the desert at its widest part was a journey of at least a year, and even at its narrowest part it was unwise to travel in a company of more than fifty people as sufficient water to supply a greater number was not to be had.

He tells us that, "in this tract neither beasts nor birds are met with because there is no kind of food for them". He goes on to say ". . . it is a well known fact that this desert is the abode of many evil spirits, which amuse travellers to their destruction with most extraordinary illusions". These "illusions" were mirages caused by layers of hot air reflecting the images of distant people and objects.

The Mountain of Salt

At Thaikan, Marco was impressed by the hills of clear fossil salt. He writes, "The hills that rise to the south of it [Thaikan], are large and lofty. They all consist of white salt, extremely hard, with which the people, to the distance of thirty days' journey round, come to provide themselves, for it is esteemed the purest that is found in the world . . . the quantity is so great that all the countries of the earth might be supplied from thence".

Afghan Shepherds

People of Kashmir
"*The natives are of a dark complexion, but by no means black; and the women although dark, are very comely . . . They are adept beyond all others in the art of magic; insomuch that they can compel their idols, although by nature dumb and deaf, to speak; they can likewise obscure the day, and perform many other miracles.*"

Buddhist Lama
"*Over 500 years before Christ was born, a young Hindu prince, tiring of court life, became a beggar and devoted his life to easing the suffering of his people. He was Guatama Buddha. He preached kindness to all living things. After his death Buddhism became one of the greatest religions of mankind. Lamas, 'the spiritual or holy ones' are the Buddhist priests of Tibet.*"

The people of Kanchow—China
"*The inhabitants had small noses and black hair, and they have no beard, save four hairs on the chin.*"

The Roof of the World

During his travels Marco crossed many mountain ranges. He says of the mountains of Badakhshan, "These mountains are exceedingly lofty, insomuch that it employs a man from morning till night to ascend to the top of them". On the summits of these mountains the ". . . air is so pure and so salubrious, that when those who dwell in the towns, find themselves attacked with fevers or other inflammatory complaints, they immediately remove thither, and remaining for three or four days in that situation, recover their health". Marco had experience of this himself, casually mentioning, ". . . having been confined by sickness, in this country, for nearly a year".

It was the mighty Pamirs, "the Roof of the World", where three mountain ranges meet, that were to prove the greatest challenge. Marco writes, "So great is the height of these mountains, that no birds are to be seen near their summits", and, ". . . that from the keenness of the air, fires when lighted do not give the same heat as in lower situations, nor produce the same effect in dressing victuals".

A later explorer refers to the ". . . frightful picture of the cold and desolation of this elevated tract, which extends for three marches [Marco says forty days] on the highest part of the country".

The Mongols

Kublai Khan

For centuries the Mongols or Tartars had lived as independent nomadic tribes wandering the steppes, south-east of Lake Baykal, in search of pasture for their cattle. They were savage, fearless people, interested only in fighting and hunting; utterly ruthless, they showed no mercy towards enemies. Their homes were beehive shaped tents called yurts, made of felt stretched over wooden frames which, mounted on wheels and dragged by oxen, followed their wandering owners; sometimes as many as twenty-two oxen were needed to pull the larger yurts. Living mainly on meat and milk, the Mongols drank vast quantities of kurmiss, fermented mare's milk.

The men were short, squat and bow-legged and were great horsemen, spending most of their lives in the saddle. They had broad smooth faces, with eyes slanted against the fierce sun and winds of the Mongolian plains.

Although they had no sovereign of their own, they paid tribute to the Khan of Chin (northern China). Temuchin, the son of a small tribal chief, worked hard to unite the separate tribes, and in 1206, at a meeting of chieftains, he was proclaimed, Genghis Khan, "Universal Lord". Asked for his annual tribute by a Chin envoy, he turned towards the south and spat. A war lasting twenty years followed, in which the Mongols captured Peking and much of northern China.

Genghis Khan and some of his warriors

The murder of some of his subjects in Persia caused Genghis Khan to assemble an army of 129,000 horsemen. With these he swept westwards across central Asia, burning and plundering as he went. When he died in 1227, his successors carried on his work of conquest, and at the time of Marco Polo the Mongolian Empire stretched from the Pacific in the east to the borders of Poland and the eastern shores of the Adriatic in the west.

The present Grand Khan Kublai, unlike Genghis, was a highly cultured man; brought up in China, he introduced many civilizing influences into the life of the Mongolian court. His luxurious palaces at Shangtu and Peking were far different from the yurts of his ancestors. In less than eighty years the scattered nomadic tribes of Mongolia had been welded into the greatest empire in the world, having complete authority over the teeming millions of Asia.

Wandering Tartars

The Palace of the Khan

The Khan's palaces at Shangtu and Peking were far more splendid
than anything Marco had seen in Europe; overwhelmed, he was lavish
in his praise of Kublai, calling him, "The great lord of lords". Peking,
the capital, was built in the form of a square, each side of which was
six miles long. It was surrounded by a high wall, with twelve gates;
the wide streets stretching the full length of the city crossed each other
at right angles. Marco tells us, ". . . no fewer than a thousand carriages
and pack horses, loaded with raw silk, make their daily entry".

In his banquet hall, which could seat 6,000, and surrounded by
golden dragons and costly tapestries, Kublai held his court. From his
raised platform, he could command a view of the entire hall, and
when he drank, musicians played and everyone knelt until he had
finished. His magicians, Tibetan Lamas in saffron robes, "caused
flagons of wine and milk to fill cups spontaneously . . . and the cups to
move through the air the distance of ten paces until they reached the
hand of the Grand Khan". The Khan held a festival each year to
celebrate his birthday, attended by 20,000 nobles all dressed in cloth
of gold.

Kublai loved hunting in the grounds of his summer palace at
Shangtu, with hawks and half tame cheetahs which rode on the back
of their keeper's horses. The Khan himself rode in a richly carved
pavilion, carried on the backs of four elephants.

The court of Kublai Khan

Courier arriving at a yamb

The Great Wall

One of the many wonders Marco saw at the court of the Khan were the black stones, which burned like charcoal and caused fires to stay alight all night.

Coal was unknown in Marco's days and he was astonished that stone dug out of mountains could be made to burn. He seemed even more astonished that the Chinese took warm baths at least three times a week, which would have been unthinkable in Venice.

Throughout Asia there was a courier system similar to the Pony Express which existed in the early days of the American West. Stations called yambs were set up at intervals of about 25 miles on all the major roads across the provinces of the Empire. Men and fresh horses were always on duty. Couriers riding day and night, from station to station could cover great distances in a short time, up to 500 miles in a day. To avoid delay, the horses had bells on their harness; on hearing the sound of these bells, the man at the next station mounted up, ready to gallop off, as if in a relay race.

Among many other things, Marco tells us of printed paper money, made from the bark of mulberry trees. Marked with the royal seal in vermilion, it could be used

Bathing

anywhere in the Khan's empire; he writes, "counterfeiting it is punished as a capital offence". Oddly enough, Marco failed to realise the importance of the fact that the money had been printed from a block. The Chinese had been using printing since the ninth century but it was to be two hundred years before it was introduced into Europe.

He also failed to mention other common features of Chinese daily life, such as the drinking of tea and the foot-binding of women, to keep their feet small and dainty.

The Great Wall of China was built 2,000 years ago to keep out the northern barbarians. Marco must have first seen it when he reached Kan-Chow. It still stands today, over 1,500 miles long, winding its way over mountains and through valleys. Originally over 20 feet high, it was wide enough for two carriages to pass or a squadron of cavalry to ride from one place to another along the wall. It is odd that not once did Marco mention seeing the Great Wall.

Servant of the Khan

Kublai Khan had great confidence in Marco's ability and sent him on many important missions. Soon he became one of the ruler's most trusted officers.

After serving as governor of the city of Yan Gui for three years, he was chosen to make an inspection tour of the imperial provinces in the name of the Khan.

Travelling throughout the Empire, he recorded many strange things. He tells of the King of Burma who built himself two pagodas, one plated with gold, the other with silver; of primitive people who used cowrie shells for money, and others who called in devil dancers to drive the evil spirits from the sick.

He also witnessed the tattooing of flowers and animals on the bodies of the Burmese. The victim was bound hand and foot, pricked with an instrument holding five needles, and indelible ink rubbed into the wounds; he ends, "many die through loss of blood".

Marco describes the Yangtze River as, "the greatest river in the world, requiring a journey of 120 days to its outlet in the sea". He was amazed at its width, remarking that it was so broad it seemed to be a sea rather than a river. At one single time he counted 15,000 boats, not including bamboo rafts.

The Shivedagon Pagoda, Burma

Yunnan

One place which seems to have impressed Marco, was Yunnan, a Chinese province on the borders of Burma. He tells us of many curious customs. "If a handsome or gentle stranger, or one who had a good shadow and good influence and valour", came to lodge in the house of one of the natives, he was killed during the night; and "this they used to do, not for money or any hatred which they had against him", but so that his soul would remain in the house to bring them good luck.

The natives hunted with lances and crossbows, and "all their arrows are poisoned". Many of them carried poison about with them, "especially those who harbour bad designs", preferring to take poison rather than be captured and tortured.

Marco tells us that the rulers were aware of this practice and to stop the poison working, '. . . an antidote is ready against the arts of these wretches".

Marco had never seen an alligator before he came to Yunnan. He writes, "Here are seen huge serpents, ten paces in length, and ten spans in the girth of the body. At the fore part, near the head, they have two short legs, having three claws like those of a tiger, with eyes larger than a fourpenny loaf, and very glaring. The jaws are wide enough to swallow a man, the teeth are large and sharp, and their whole appearance is so formidable, that neither man nor any kind of animal can approach them without terror". During the great heat of the daytime, "they lurk in caverns", coming out at night to hunt, and any animal "whether tiger, wolf, or any other they lay hold of and devour". After

Hunting alligators

eating, the alligators drag themselves along their trails to the river; here the natives dig pits, "... and fix into the ground several pieces of wood, armed with sharp iron spikes, which they cover with sand in such a manner as not to be perceptible".

The animals fall onto the spikes and are speedily killed. "The crows, as soon as they perceive them to be dead, set up their scream; and this serves as a signal to the hunters." The gall of the alligator is, "most highly esteemed in medicine. In cases of the bite of a mad dog, a pennyweight of it dissolved in wine, is administered. . . . The meat is in great demand, the natives paying for it with cowrie shells".

Hangchow

Marco found Hangchow like Venice but very much larger; instead of one central market it had ten, each being half a mile long and half a mile wide.

The city itself was, "an hundred miles in circuit", and its endless canals were spanned by 12,000 bridges. "Those which are thrown over the principal canals and are connected with the main streets, have arches so high, and are built with so much skill, that vessels with their masts can pass under them, whilst at the same time, carts and horses are passing over their heads."

We are told that the Great Khan tolerated neither beggars nor vagabonds in Hangchow, for if the city guards, "by day see any poor man who because of being crippled cannot work, they make him go to stay in the hospitals, of which there is an infinitely large number throughout the city. And if he be sound of body they compel him to do some work".

Some idea of the size of the city can be gained from the amount of pepper used in one day. According to one of Kublai's Customs Officers, "the daily amount was forty-three loads, each load being two-hundred-and-forty-three pounds".

The Homeward Voyage

After seventeen years in the Khan's service, the Polos began to think of returning to Venice, but Kublai wanted them to remain in his realm, "on no condition in the world could they leave it".

At last, with "great displeasure on his countenance", the Khan reluctantly agreed to the Polos sailing to Persia with the Princess Cocachin. In 1292 they set sail from the port of Zayton in a convoy of fourteen great ships, each having four masts and a crew of two to three hundred sailors. They were built of fir and pine and contained as many as sixty cabins. Marco gives an interesting description of the watertight compartments of these ships, ". . . so if by chance it happens that the ship is damaged in any place either if it strikes on a rock or a whale fish . . . the water entering through the hole will run to the bottom, which is never filled with any other things. Then the sailors seek out in what compartment the ship is damaged and then that compartment is emptied into others, for the water cannot pass from one compartment into the other, so strongly are they enclosed. And then they repair the ship there . . ."

The voyage to Persia took two years, during which many of the ships were either wrecked or swept with scurvy and sickness. Of the six hundred passengers who set out from China, only eighteen reached the Persian port of Hormuz alive.

Pearl Fishing

Before describing the voyage, Marco writes of the unsuccessful attempts made by the Mongols to invade Japan, and the Japanese warriors who could not be wounded by iron swords, because of the precious stones, "enchanted by the devil's art", which they wore under the skin of their right arm. However, the precious stones were of no avail; "the barons caused them to be beaten with clubs of thick wood, and they died at once".

He tells how the people of Japan had much gold, and buried their dead each with a great pearl in his mouth. It was stories like this that fired Columbus with his zeal for discovery and caused him to carry a copy of Marco's travels, heavily annotated, on his first voyage across the Atlantic.

He found the people of Sumatra were cannibals, and he dug a large deep ditch and built five "Towers" as a defence against them. They later became friendly and supplied the travellers with fish, coconuts and other food. He also saw a rhinoceros for the first time, though he calls it a "Unicorn", despite the fact that it had two horns. He also refers to the "tailed" men of Lambrai—probably these were orang-outangs. The people of the Andaman Islands he describes as

having heads and faces like dogs. In Ceylon he saw, "the largest ruby that is to be found in all the world".

In India he learned that, "he who drinks wine is not accepted as a witness, nor is he who navigates the sea, . . . for they are desperate, unreliable people".

Marco gives a most interesting account of the pearl fishing off Malabar. In waters from ten to twelve fathoms deep, the natives dive for oysters throughout the whole day, "these they bring up in bags made of netting that are fastened about their bodies. . . . the Fishery commences in the month of April and lasts till the middle of May".

As a protection against sharks, the pearl merchants, "are accompanied by certain enchanters belonging to a class of Brahmans who, by means of their diabolical art, have the power of constraining and stupefying these fish, so as to prevent them from doing mischief". At night the charm was lifted so as to prevent poachers from diving for the oysters. Marco concludes, "the enchanters are likewise profound adepts in the art of fascinating all kinds of beasts and birds".

Arrival at Venice

Coming at last to Hormuz on the Persian Gulf, they left Princess Cocachin with the new Khan, and continued their journey to Venice overland. They finally reached the city in 1295, twenty-four years after they had left it.

Although Marco says nothing of their return, many stories and legends have built up over the years, which may or may not be true. No one recognized these ragged strangers dressed in the "fashion of the Tartars", and who had "indescribably something of the Tartar

in their aspect and way of speech, having almost forgotten the Venetian tongue". Reluctantly, their relatives were persuaded to allow them to enter their house. Legend has it that the Polos had a fortune in precious jewels sewn into their clothes, which they revealed to their doubting relatives and friends at a great banquet.

Marco had difficulty in getting people to believe his stories of the Khan's court, and the wonders and immense riches of China. After his death he became a comic character in Venetian puppet shows called "Il Milione", the man of the millions.

The Venetians doubted many of Marco's stories and thought that he made everything larger than life.

Capture at Sea

Marco Polo, after only a few months at home, began to get restless. Venice being once again at war with "Genoa the Superb", her great trade rival, he decided to equip a war galley and join a fleet sailing to attack the Genoese. However, the Venetian fleet was heavily defeated and Marco himself captured.

He was then imprisoned in an underground room in the Palazzo di San Gorgio in Genoa, together with many other officers and merchants, being spared the dungeons, which were the fate of the "common sailors and fighting men". Here he met Rusticiano of Pisa, who wrote down the story of Marco's travels for him, beginning his account, "Ye Emperors, kings, dukes, marquises, earls and knights, and all other people desirous of knowing the diversities of the races of mankind".

After peace had been declared in 1299, Marco returned to Venice, married and finally settled down to the humdrum life of a prosperous merchant. Little is known of him until his death in 1324.

Although during his lifetime his "Description of the World" was treated with disbelief, it was nevertheless very popular and in great demand as a collection of stories. The original manuscript, written in old French, was copied into many languages, Venetian, Spanish, German, Bohemian, and so on. In all, a hundred and nineteen manuscripts have been found. It was first printed in Germany in 1477, and since then it has been printed many times and translated into many languages.

Most of Marco's writings have since been proved to be true, but here and there he appears to accept odd medieval fables as the truth; for instance, referring to mirages he writes, "Sometimes likewise during the day those spirits assume the appearance of their travelling companions, who address them by their name and endeavour to conduct them out of their proper road". Such was the general disbelief during his lifetime, that it was a hundred years before the results of his travels began to appear on maps. Gradually people began to accept his findings, until it was finally realised that his travels were some of the greatest feats of exploration of all time.

Venetian and Genoese war galleys

Index

Venice

Constantinople   *Black Sea*   GEORGIA

ARMENIA   Trebizond

Mediterranean Sea   Ayas   Erzurum   Baku

Caspian Sea

Acre   Y. Tunocain   Balkh   Kash

Jerusalem   PERSIA   THE PAMIRS   Kh

AFRICA   Baghdad   Salt Desert   AFGHANISTAN

Kerman

ARABIA   Persian Gulf   Hormuz

Indian Ocean